MALIK

MAX

JENNA

FUMI

MARISOL

JAKE

First Food Fight This Fall

and Other School Poems

by Marilyn Singer • illustrated by Sachiko Yoshikawa

STERLING

New York / London

Acknowledgments

Thanks to Steve Aronson; Michele Coppola Ames; Donna O'Donnell Figurski; Francis Heaney; my wonderful editor, Meredith Mundy Wasinger; stellar senior designer, Lauren Rille; and the rest of the super crew at Sterling. —M.S.

A million thanks to Namiko Rudi, Mikako Sullivan, and Sarah Waller for your great help. —S.Y.

To the extraordinary
Lee Bennett Hopkins
—M.S.

To Pao
—S.Y.

POEMS

FIRST DAY
by Dylan

Click.
The new driver has turned
 our old bus into a parade float—
  flowers on the bumpers,
  balloons on the roof,
  banners across both sides.
Yay! they say.
First day!
And one by one (or two or three)
we hop, jump, climb, bump on.
Click.
There's Marisol with her Top Girl tee shirt,
Cory with a cobra on his cap.
Click.
Kwan hiding behind his notebook,
Laksmi hiding behind her hair.

YAY! FIRST

4

Click.
Jake in India, colored pencils sketching a rain forest,
Max in the clouds, predicting a sunny day.
Those twins, Jenna and Abigail, identically different,
with fast feet or careful hands.
That pair, Amy and Malik, differently identical,
always lagging and ragging.
Fumi wiggling her shoulders
to some music no one else can hear.
And me,
taking pictures
without a camera.
Click click.

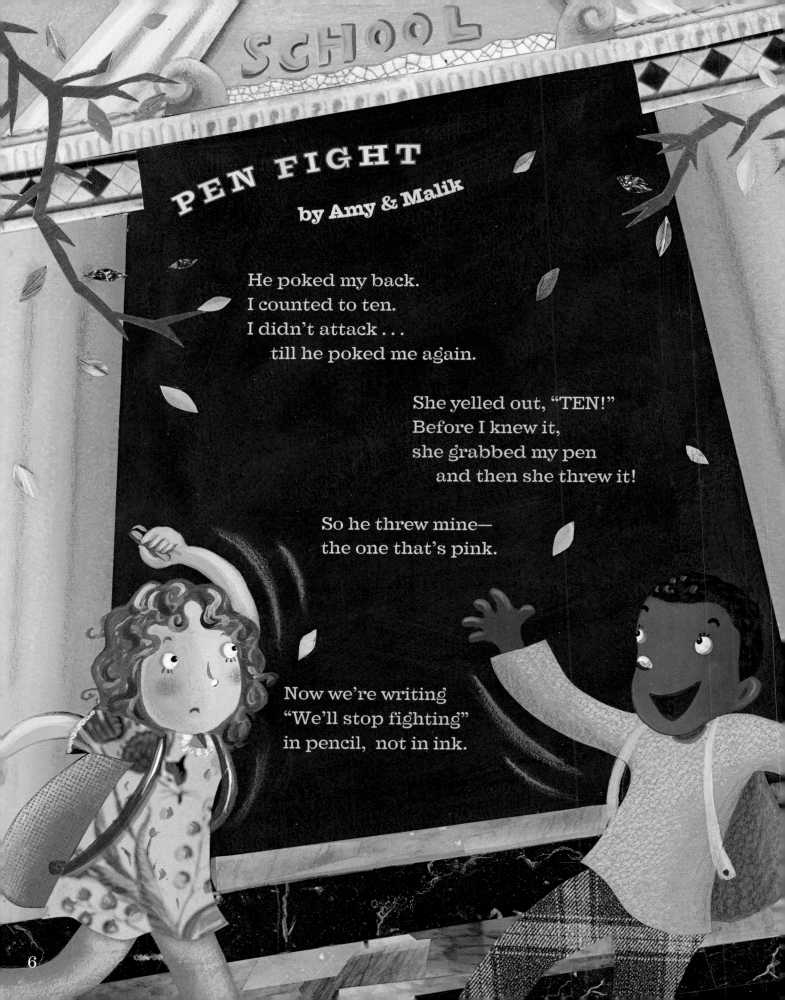

PEN FIGHT

by Amy & Malik

He poked my back.
I counted to ten.
I didn't attack . . .
    till he poked me again.

                She yelled out, "TEN!"
                Before I knew it,
                she grabbed my pen
                    and then she threw it!

                So he threw mine—
                the one that's pink.

Now we're writing
"We'll stop fighting"
in pencil, not in ink.

SCHOOL

6

CLEANING ERASERS
by Kwan

I love
to erase the
board. To make today's words
and numbers smear, then disappear
from here.

I clap
the erasers
out the open window.
Watch out below—lessons heading
your way!

WHAT I THINK OF POETRY
by Laksmi

Poetry makes me
sleepy: lullaby words in
a warm, quiet room.

SPELLING
by Marisol

Test time, and I cannot spell *beak*,
climb, *speech*, *November*.
It's the crazy words I remember—
the ones Ms. Mundy gives each week:
grunion, *bunion*, *snooze*, *physique*,
succotash, *Zamboni*, *folderol*, *flounce*—
wacky stuff that is fun to pronounce.
My parents don't get it. They think it's absurd—
how do I get *quetzal* right,
but still mess up on *bird*?

grunion
folderol
snooze

MATH
by Cory

I can ski right down a mountain,
I can sail across a lake.
I make really good lasagna
and delicious chocolate cake.
I am not afraid of spiders,
and one time I touched a snake!
But I will not do math on the board—
I might make a mistake.

TAG

by Jenna & Abigail

I'm the very best at tag.
It's my great claim to fame.
I can zig and I can zag.
I'm the very best at tag.
I'll let the cat out of the bag—
my *dog* taught me the game.
I'm the very best at tag.
It's my great claim to fame.

My classmates call me *Snail*.
At tag, I'm always *It*.
My real name's Abigail.
My classmates call me *Snail*.
I wish they'd let me bail.
I'd much prefer to sit.
My classmates call me *Snail*.
At tag, I'm always *It*.

11

THE CLASS I HATE

by Fumi

A-tisket, a-tasket,
don't wanna shoot a basket,
or join a baseball team,
or walk the balance beam.
Would I care to climb a rope,
run, or tumble? One word: nope!
I don't even like to swim.
Guess what class I hate.
It's gym!

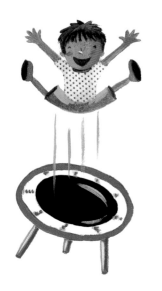

ART
by Jake

I'm drawing a picture with colorful chalks—
   a tangly jungle, a tiger that stalks—
right on the ground in the busy schoolyard.
   (The jungle is easy; the tiger is hard.)
I'm drawing a picture I know will not stay—
   tomorrow the rain's gonna wash it away.
But I'll do another, or seven, or ten
   when the sun says it's time to draw tigers again!

WHERE THE CUSTODIAN CAN GO

by Cory & Marisol

Behind that door
there are giggles and chatter,
water running, the smell of perfume.
Behind that door
there's a whole lot of trouble—
if I peeked in, I would meet my **DOOM**.
'Cause Mr. Monticello
with his mop and broom
is the only guy allowed inside
that freaky girls' restroom.

Behind that door
there are snorts and clatter,
water flooding, the occasional
BOOM.
Behind that door
there are boys causing trouble—
they don't go there to chat or groom.
Poor Mr. Monticello
with his mop and broom.
What messes has he found
in the wacky boys' restroom?

MARYLOU MUNDY
by Everyone

Makes adjectives intriguing
And calculation really cool.
Rides a bike that's sunlight
Yellow, rain or shine, each day to school.
Likes lizards, snakes, and spiders
(**O**nce she owned a blue-lined skink!).
Uses mushrooms to make pictures.
_arks our tests with orange ink.
Understands when you act silly,
Never yells when you're a pest.
Don't you wish you had our teacher?
Yes, she IS the very best!

SANDWICH TRADES
by Max

Jake doesn't like peanut butter and jelly,
egg salad, meatballs, any cheese that's smelly,
bologna on a roll, tuna fish on rye,
chicken nuggets, nachos, even pizza pie.
But bean curd with sprouts or dandelion greens,
marinated mushrooms, oily sardines,
ripe avocado sliced on whole wheat,
and artichoke pâté are things he *loves* to eat—
and what my mother makes!
So each day we exchange.
I'm glad to have a friend
whose favorite foods are strange!

FIRST FOOD FIGHT THIS FALL

by Fumi, Jake, Max, Abigail & Jenna

A cafeteria ballad—
it started with tossed salad.
Was it Amy or Malik
who let out a shriek
then wound up and threw?
(That lettuce really flew!
We're glad it wasn't stew!)

Food fight, food fight,
free for all!
First wild food fight of the fall!

18

INDOOR STORM

by Dylan

Even Max couldn't have predicted
    shredded-lettuce rain and cherry-tomato hail.
You have to look hard to spot the carrots
    in Amy's red hair,
but everyone can see the cucumbers on Malik's head
    like strange soggy flowers,
    waiting for our principal to pick.

While Jake studies the splotches
  of dressing on his shirt,
  probably wondering what paints
  he'd have to mix to get that color,
Kwan and Laksmi, Cory and Marisol quietly begin
  to dab, wipe, sweep, and scrub,
until Mr. Monticello, with just one sigh,
comes with mop, pail, and sponge
  to erase every last trace
of the indoor storm.

WHEN MS. MUNDY READ US A POEM

by Laksmi & Kwan

I fell asleep as
usual. Only this time
I dreamed of flowers.

silver clouds dew drops

On the
grayest fall day,
all the maples outside
were bare, but in our room cherry
trees bloomed.

towering

22

THE CLASS I LOVE
by Fumi

Hickory, dickory, dock,
hurry up, hurry up, clock!
I want the time to pass
so I can get to class.
Here's the crazy thing:
I can cha-cha, rumba, swing,
do merengue, salsa, too.
There's no dance that I can't do.
Yes, I know what I once said.
But now I love, love, LOVE Phys. Ed.!

FIRST SNOW
by Dylan

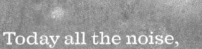

Today all the noise,
    all the squeaking swings, thunking basketballs,
    slapping jump ropes, thwapping sneakers,
all the buzzing, laughing, shrieking,
all the running, shoving, hide-and-seeking
      stopped.

Posing for a perfect photograph,
we looked up, still and silent,
heads tilted, mouths open wide,
to catch the first snowflakes of December
on the last outdoor recess of the year.

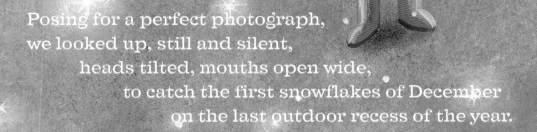

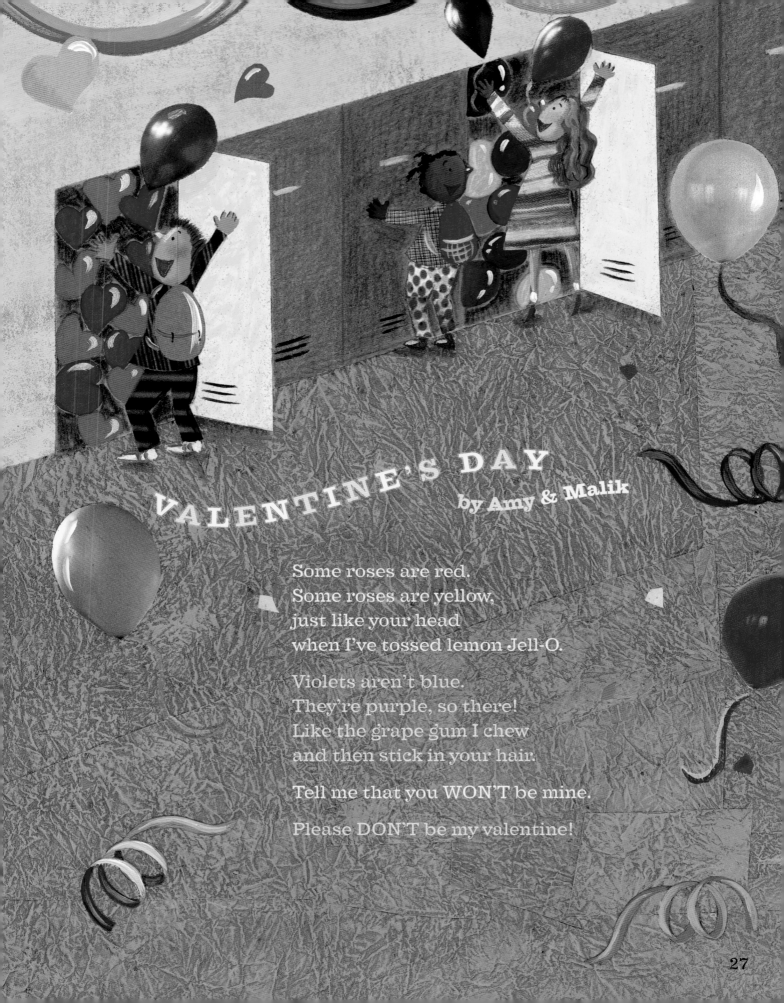

VALENTINE'S DAY

by Amy & Malik

Some roses are red.
Some roses are yellow,
just like your head
when I've tossed lemon Jell-O.

Violets aren't blue.
They're purple, so there!
Like the grape gum I chew
and then stick in your hair.

Tell me that you WON'T be mine.

Please DON'T be my valentine!

SCIENCE FAIR
by Max

High pressure, low pressure, water in the air.
Photographs of clouds. Today's the science fair.
What is my project? It's meteorology.
That's a barometer—simple technology.
See, I planned to find out if we get more A's
when the sun is shining or on rainy days.
Did Ms. Mundy help? Yes, she gave lots of quizzes
just to help prove that on sunny days we're whizzes!
I stood up for science, but now my class protests,
"*Pooh* on weather, *Foo* on Max, and *Boo* on all those tests!"

FIRST PRIZE FRIEND
by Jake

Hip hooray for rain clouds, hip hooray for sun!
Hip hooray for my friend Max, 'cause his project won
first prize at the science fair! Man, that's really great!
Bet you anything it takes first place in the state!
Scientists need data—quite a large amount.
All those spelling tests we took?
Good news! They don't count!
Well, not unless we want them to.
Isn't that too cool?
Plus now we spell much better
than anyone in school!
So come on everybody—let's give Max a break.
And celebrate with slices of his mother's kiwi cake.

FOR BEANS!
by Jenna & Abigail

I'm good at tag; I'm bad with seeds.
My bean plant will not sprout.
I tried to give it what it needs.
I'm good at tag; I'm bad with seeds.
I couldn't grow a bunch of weeds.
No leaf is peeping out.
I'm good at tag; I'm bad with seeds.
My bean plant will not sprout.

I grew the tallest string bean plant.
Ms. Mundy says I have the knack.
I got a green thumb from my aunt.
I grew the tallest string bean plant.
I did what my twin sister can't.
Instead of *Snail*, they'll call me *Jack*.
I grew the tallest string bean plant.
Ms. Mundy says I have the knack.

SPRING ME!
by Kwan & Laksmi

Silly
bee bumping
the window, let's
trade places. You want to come
in and work. I want to go out
and play.

What woke me? It might
have been a robin. It might
have been a poem.

31

FIELD TRIP
by Jake

Look at this painting, that color, this line.
Look at that tiger, so different from mine.
Look at the walls, at the ceiling, the floor.
Art, everywhere! In the next room there's more!
Boats in the harbor, a girl with a cup . . .
Will I be an artist when I grow up?
Will they hang my pictures where people can see 'em
when they take a trip to this super museum?

WATER FIGHT

by Amy & Malik

After kickball I was sweaty.
My face was warm and pink.
I went up to the fountain
　　to get a long cool drink.

I was there before her.
I made the fountain squirt
water on her cheeks and chin,
　　water down her shirt.

The next time I was waiting,
I got him up the nose.
Ms. Mundy frowned and asked him
　　if he'd wrestled with a hose.

Principal Wasnusky,
we plan to call a truce.
Today instead of water,
　　we promise we'll have juice.

PERFECT SCORE
by Marisol

I did it. Amazing!
My eyes were glazing
over, just as I feared.
And then *lettuce* appeared
like magic in my brain.
Also *rabbit, turtle, waffles, drain.*
I could practically smell them.
I *knew* I could *spell* them!
Today came the proof. I did it! I did!
An orange one *hunderd*—
    (I mean, one hun*dred*.)

ON THE BOARD

by Cory

I did it. Amazing!
I found myself raising
my hand although I was scared.
But I did it—I dared
do that math on the board.
I multiplied, added, and, yes, then I scored!
"Twelve!" I declared. But the answer was five.
I knew it, I blew it. Still, I guess I'll survive.
Miss Mundy agreed it was good that I tried.
And it *would* have been right
if I'd thought to divide!

CLASS PICTURE
by Dylan

The photographer is late.
We are itchy from waiting and new clothes.
(Max is even wearing a tie!)
Ms. Mundy takes out her camera
     and hands it to me.
"Till he gets here," she says.
I line them all up.
"Say *cheese*," I command.
"Muenster." Malik doesn't smile.
"Say *shredded wheat*."
"Cornflakes." Amy doesn't smile either.
"Say '*Dylan is goofy. His hair is too poofy.*'"
(Which is true.)
The whole class laughs.
Amy and Malik roll their eyes.
"Cheese," they say.
Click.
"Gotcha!" I grin.
And later on the computer
we find out that
I did.

37

FIELD DAY

by Jenna & Abigail

The park! The park! Our favorite place!
On Field Day everybody wins!
Such grass and trees and all this space!
The park! The park! Our favorite place!
We aced it—the three-legged race!
Who could beat a pair of twins?
The park! The park! Our favorite place!
On Field Day everybody wins!

FINISH

LAST, FIRST

by Cory & Marisol

Last hurry-up bell.
Last pledge to the flag.
Last big words to spell.
Last wild game of tag.

Last girls' restroom pass.
Last hundred I scored.
Last secrets in class.
Last math on the board.

by Amy & Malik

Last bubblegum stash.
Last lesson we're taught.
Last fountain to splash.
Last chance to get caught.

Last books in my pack.
Last race down the hall.
Last snack in a sack.
Last food fight till fall!

by Kwan & Laksmi

$$\frac{5}{11} + \frac{3}{11} = ?$$

Last board to erase.
Last pencil I've found.
Last chairs all in place.
Last hugs all around.

Last read-aloud poem.
Last wish we could stay.
Last loud bus ride home.
Last busy school day.

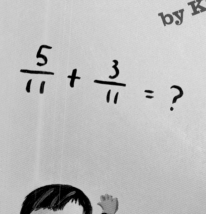

by Max

First chance to sleep late.
First day it's too warm.
First do-nothing date.
First great thunderstorm!

by Abigail & Jenna

First race to the beach.
First green beans to pick.
First sweet-tasting peach.
First jellyfish—ick!

by Jake

First shell in my hand.
First crab for a pet.
First sketch in the sand.
First chance to get wet.

by Fumi

First dome tent to pitch.
First making s'mores.
First bug bites that itch.
First dancing outdoors.

by Dylan

First riding the waves.
First boogie-board tricks.
First strange ocean caves.
First cool travel pix.

by All

First star in the sky.
First "Look, it's still light!"
First bright firefly.
First long summer night.

STERLING and the distinctive Sterling logo
are registered trademarks of Sterling Publishing Co., Inc.

Library of Congress Cataloging-in-Publication Data

Singer, Marilyn.
First food fight this fall and other school poems / by Marilyn Singer ;
illustrated by Sachiko Yoshikawa.
p. cm.
ISBN: 978-1-4027-4145-6
1. School children—Poetry. I. Yoshikawa, Sachiko, ill. II. Title.

PS3569.I546F58 2008
811'.54—dc22
2007043386

10 9 8 7 6 5 4 3 2 1

Published by Sterling Publishing Co., Inc.
387 Park Avenue South, New York, NY 10016
Text © 2008 by Marilyn Singer
Illustrations © 2008 by Sachiko Yoshikawa

Distributed in Canada by Sterling Publishing
c/o Canadian Manda Group, 165 Dufferin Street
Toronto, Ontario, Canada M6K 3H6
Distributed in the United Kingdom by GMC Distribution Services
Castle Place, 166 High Street, Lewes, East Sussex, England BN7 1XU
Distributed in Australia by Capricorn Link (Australia) Pty. Ltd.
P.O. Box 704, Windsor, NSW 2756, Australia

Printed in China

The artwork was prepared using acrylics, pastels and collage.
Designed by Lauren Rille

Sterling ISBN 978-1-4027-4145-6

For information about custom editions, special sales, premium and
corporate purchases, please contact Sterling Special Sales Department
at 800-805-5489 or specialsales@sterlingpublishing.com.

ABIGAIL

KWAN

DYLAN

CORY

LAKSMI

AMY